Letters to Mother Earth

Ferguson & Fiore

PO Box 71
Kilauea, HI 96754
www.LettersToMother.org

Printed in the United States of America

ISBN-13: 978-0-578-42732-4

Contents

Dear Reader,

Have you ever wondered if the planet is real, if she's alive?

Have you ever called her … Mother?
Have you ever marveled at the natural beauty of this Blue Planet?
Have you ever had a moment of awe, in nature, where you felt really connected?
Have you ever felt a deep hurt - seeing the damage we are doing to the Earth?
Do you have a deep feeling - a knowing - that there must be a better way?

This book is a collection of letters to our mother, Mother Earth. The letters range from apologies, to acknowledgements, to questions and realizations. She has always shown us, taught us, and demonstrated to us - the ways, the perfection, and the wonder of nature.

This is not an ordinary book. It is not intended to convey information or convince you of a truth. The purpose of this book is to provide the reader with stories, tools, thoughts and experiences that encourage a deeper connection with the Spirit of Mother Earth.

The intent is to inspire an expanded awareness and to make a positive difference in how we live and how we relate to the planet, to ourselves, to each other, to Universal Consciousness. It feels like we are in a time of awakening.

These letters are written to the Divine Feminine, the Spirit of Mother Earth.
She seems so accessible compared to the Divine Masculine. Our ideas about God
have become so divisive, so disassembled, that we are fighting and killing each other
over our differences. We don't seem to have the ability to view ourselves as a global
humanity, and cultures all over the world have become so entrenched in their beliefs
that it is unlikely that we will come together around our ideas about God. But across
cultures, across the planet and throughout time, we have had a very common
understanding, or knowing, of Mother Earth. Universally, she is nurturing, she is
loving, she is accessible and she is inclusive. Ultimately, the Divine Feminine and the
Divine Masculine are all part of the same, but for now … it seems like the Mother of
All Life is a great place to start to have a conversation.

Connecting to Mother Nature can take you to a place where everything slows down.
Slow down … as you read … and "feel" these letters with your heart. Feel beneath
the old story of separation that we have been telling ourselves. When we slow down
we get to feel; feel connected. Connected to spirit, connected to our heart, connected
to nature. In this connection is a new way of looking at things and the beginning of
a new kind of relationship between us and nature. A new way of experiencing and
relating to—her.

Dear Mother,

It is sometimes hard for me to remember that you are actually an amazing blue water planet, with a beautiful atmosphere, and that your oceans somehow retain their form as you rotate through space. It's easy for us to not even see you, because you literally *are* our world. As long as we have been humanity we have gazed up at the stars in the night sky and looked "out" from our perspective here on Earth. But the first time we saw you from space, we all had to take a step back and catch our breath. Our hearts swelled with appreciation and wonder, and we had this overwhelming feeling of awe. We experienced a feeling of pride, and gratitude that we get to live here - that this is our home. We saw just how beautiful you really are.

For the first time - we were able to look "back" … at ourselves … as a global humanity. It helped us to realize that we are all in the same boat and it made us aware that we have to protect this beautiful planet. It made us realize that the air, the water, the land, and all natural resources are precious.

Compared to every other planet that we can see, with powerful telescopes probing the night sky, Earth is very unique, very beautiful and very alive. There is nothing "out there" in space that even comes close. It's hard to image anyplace more spectacular, more perfect. *Thank you* for sustaining us and for being our Mother here on this amazing planet.

The other planets are probably alive too, but there you are... hanging in the blackness of space in full bloom, vibrant and alive. Your atmosphere seems to be inhaling and exhaling white art forms across your blue skies. Were pure water falls from the clouds - flows in river veins, shapes mountains, greens the land and grows colorful flowers and food. A magnificent, living expression of life, You are the mother, the provider, the nurturer of all life—it is the foundation for all life here.

Mother - we know that we get moving too fast. We rarely stop and put you into perspective. Sometimes it seems that we are just too close. We literally can't see the forrest for the trees. Earth is so amazing within the context of space. We have never seen anything like you.

We appreciate all you have given us and we are beginning to understand that we have a responsibility to you. We recognize that our existence is having an impact. We are degrading the very things that make this planet special. The water on this planet is what makes it so unique and it is a little scary to think about how fragile it is. The range of temperatures for the Earth to remain a water planet is mind boggling small — barely a needle blip within the vast temperature range of space.

The air in your beautiful blue atmosphere is also fragile and we are affecting that too. We now realize that the air we breathe today is the same air the dinosaurs breathed. You have such an amazing system to cleanse the air, the water, and the land. Your fields, your oceans, your mountains, are just so perfect and the only things that are not perfect, are things we created in our unawareness.

Even when our children make messes, we try to both clean up the mess and help them to understand that they have to be responsible because if the mess gets too big to clean up, then our environment gets unlivable. We have to take responsibility.

Mother, it feels like we are at that point. It feels like our messes are getting so big that if we don't start cleaning them up, our home will get unlivable. We are living in the most beautiful place — with natural beauty and elegance almost beyond our ability to imagine. A place of infinite perfection and balance where are things, all life, lives in harmony — and has been doing so for time longer than we can even comprehend. It is tragic to think that in the last 50 or 60 years, we are literally destroying it.

We are welcome guests here, we are your children and yet it seems like we have soiled our beautiful home. Some of us act like we don't even care. It's like we are not even aware. We need to clean up our messes, and not just the physical messes we have made, but also the messes we have made in our own minds.

To the degree that we don't know, don't care, and don't see, we have told ourselves that it doesn't matter. Someone else will clean it up, someone else will take responsibility, someone else will care.

That's not working.

We are so sorry. We are ready to change. We are ready to take responsibility for ourselves and for our actions. We are ready to listen. We are ready to learn.

Our collective future generations are depending on us to figure out how to live here with grace and ease — rather than in conflict, and causing harm.

We know that we can't continue down this path of expansion and consumption without at least having a conversation or a plan for how we are going to exist on this planet long-term — as a global humanity.

It starts with us. What we do …. matters
and there are big pieces that we can control
our Thoughts, our Awareness, our Intention, our Appreciation.

The energy that's inside each of us is very powerful
Individually, we can make a difference
Collectively, we are an enormous life force in the Universe!

We are going to find a better way.

Moon With A View

This thing is blowing my mind
I can see Africa, Europe, the polar ice caps
It's all passing and turning beneath me
Suspended in space
Simply watching the Earth roll by

How majestic
How real
How beautiful

I think about nations
I think about cities
I think about people
I think about us

Here I am on this barren moonscape

Watching, imagining, wishing I could
Put my feet on her soil
My body in her water
My eyes on her beauty

I wonder how many other empty moons and planets there are

I wonder why we don't see what I see - right now

I will not take theEarth for granted
I acknowledge and appreciate her
She is Alive

Dear Mother,

Thank you for letting us call this amazing planet — Home.

Thank you for …. pretty much everything
    our air
    our water
    our food
    our world.

Thank you for connecting with us.

Thank you for being patient with us. It has taken us a long time to begin to
re-awaken. Thank you for showing us how to silence our minds and drop
into a real feeling experience.

We feel grateful when we spend time in nature, spend time with the
mountains, spend time with the rivers — spend time with our true selves.
You reach us and bring us into alignment and harmony with you and we
get to be at ease — in the perfection of the Universe.

When we are in nature, when we are part of a living surrounding,
it's easier to quiet our minds and let our distractions disappear.
We can drop into a real feeling experience — feeling a connection with you.

Thank you for this gift —
the simple ability to *feel* and
be connected to nature, connected to the ocean,
the woods, the birds, and all life on Earth.
Connected to your true self, connected to spirit, connected to each other.

This idea that everything is connected
gives us a new way of looking at things,
the beginning of a new kind of relationship with ourselves
and with you.

Dear Mother,

We are sorry. We are living in the most beautiful, magical place—with all things, and all life, living in harmony and natural perfection—and in just the last 50 or 60 years, we are causing impacts on levels beyond our ability to measure or understand

We have told ourselves that you are so vast that our impacts don't matter. We have fooled ourselves—to the point that we don't know, don't care, and don't see. We are not willing to take responsibility.

We bought into this unsettling idea that it's okay to harm the planet as long as there's enough money involved.
We have pretty much decided that
growth, economic expansion and profits, are
more important than saving our natural world.

We've been telling ourselves that you're not real—that what we are doing doesn't matter and now we are finding ourselves at a kind of tipping point.

We can either continue the path we're on,
degrading the planet and living on the brink of nuclear war, or
find a way to change things before its too late.

We all have a deep knowing that the path we're on is not right with you,
We are all feeling like there must be a better way.

We have to wake up, learn to feel, and take responsibility for ourselves.

Many of us have lost our connection with you. We got so wrapped up in the smallness of our own lives, we bought into the idea that we are separate and spent too much time in our minds and not enough time in our hearts. We forgot how to really see you, really appreciate you and acknowledge you.

We told ourselves that everything would be solved by technological advances. We should be getting more connected, but instead, we focus more and more on what divides us.

Humanity that came before us had no perspective on these things. They lived in a world of unlimited resources. We may be the first generations to grasp the impact of what we are doing and see the end of what we thought was an "endless" supply of clean air, good water, food, and natural resources.

Deep down, we've all known that we can't keep recklessly consuming and now, we are becoming more aware. We are now choosing to feel our way forward with both our hearts and minds, in deep reverence for all that is and all you have provided.

Mother, with this new awareness and connection we have been able to see you clearly—for who you really are. We love you and will protect you, just like you have always protected us—your children. We appreciate our connection and all that you give us. We are beginning to be aware that we have a responsibility to you. We are sorry we didn't see it sooner.

Is She Real

She definitely has energy
She seems to be breathing
She is covered with life
Her rivers are like veins
Her forests like lungs
She can give life ....and
She can take it away

We get to feel her
We get to connect
Real .....in fleeting moments
Hard to describe her as unreal, after
Experiencing connection

She is made of the same stuff as us
We are all energy
The Earth is energy
We see her, we hear her
We feel her when our vibrations match

She has a field of consciousness
It's beautiful in its perfection,
It's intention,
It's expression, and
We can connect with it

That's how she communicates
She doesn't use words or thoughts
and it's not what we're taught

She is beautiful, and
We call her ....Mother

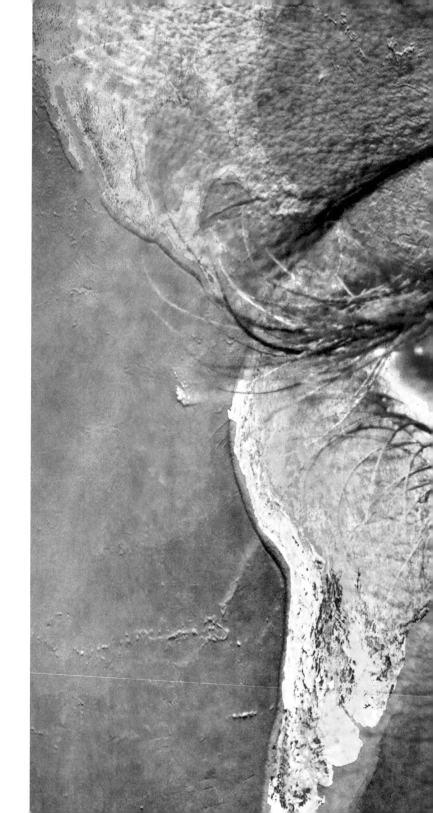

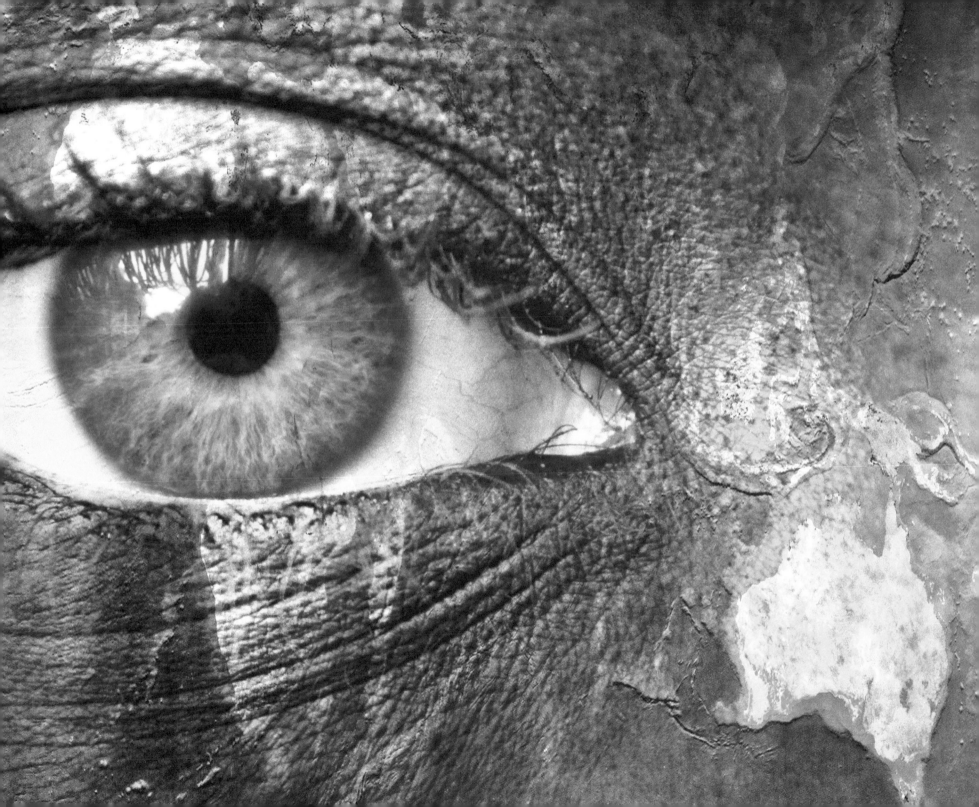

Dear Mother,

Where did we go wrong, how did we get so disconnected?
Maybe our systems of culture, governance, education, and organized religion have led us to this place of disconnectedness. We created this economic system that places emphasis on obtaining and getting and consuming. It focuses on the outer experience rather than the inner relationship that many indigenous cultures understood. This system distracts us and keeps us away from our relationship with you, and prevents us from understanding our connection.

Our education system is built on the foundation of our parents and their parents' parents. We are teaching our children about the world that used to be. They viewed the world as limitless and weren't aware that we could deplete resources, degrade the water and contaminate the air. But now we know—humanity causes a *lot* of destruction. Our education system has not caught up with what we know about how to live in the world.

Our organized religions also contribute to our disconnectedness. Some of the worlds' religions taught us that we are born with original sin— from actions that happened at the very beginnings of humanity. According to this story, we did something wrong that somehow angered God and now all of humanity must live disconnected.

Further, we allowed someone to come between us and our relationship with God. No wonder we feel separated from ourselves, from each other, and from you. Organized religion tells us "Man shall have dominion over the Earth." We have taken that old belief as a license to treat the earth like a resource to be used up. But, what if it simply means that we possess a higher love to spread over the plants and animals and that we have a responsibility to be care givers to the planet, as opposed to only being takers.

Our modern culture also contributes to our separation. We have been programmed to believe that happiness is "out there." If we do more, obtain more,
get more—then... we will be happy. The media has programmed us to strive
for money, cars, houses and clothes. We all feel the day-to-day pressures of
society and our peers
and the cultural impressions and expectation that we ought to
be wealthy, successful people. The First Peoples all lived with
inner-wealth, with reverence for—and in harmony with—nature.
The Industrial Revolution brought great technological advances
and conveniences that have the ability to connect us, but the
problem is, they are mostly distracting us. We are living in an era
when technology, entertainment and stimulation consume our time and energy.
We imagine that there is no time for us to have a
relationship with ourselves, let alone a relationship with you.

We are putting our relationship with ourselves, with you and with
God in the hands of others, thereby feeling like we are unaccountable. We have
pretty much blindly participated in this—and while
nobody ever meant for anything bad to happen, now we can
begin to see what we created. There must be a better way!

Dear Mother,

I have, at times, felt the connection to you. Really *felt* it. We have all felt that way, even if only for a fleeting moment. These moments are unmistakeable. They can make you stop what you are doing …and when we experience that connection with you, it's hard to feel anything but appreciation ….and gratitude.

We seem to have these moments of connection with the peacefulness of a sunset, or when we take the time to stop in the woods, by a river, on a mountain, or anywhere in nature. It's like we remember something ….real.

How beautiful that there's something to be connected to. That the Earth has consciousness and a soothing energy.

Why don't we feel that connection with you all the time? Maybe it's our mind that checks out of the connection because we think it's too good to be true, that you could really be connected to an energy of love.

But you are always there, and we all have the ability to experience you; nothing is required except to do it.

We love to seek out an elevated, perched perspective so we can take in more of you. People are drawn to climb to the tops of your mountains, to look out over your oceans from the edges of cliffs. We are attracted to the top floors of buildings, just to get that view, that feeling, that sense of awe where you are so present, so overwhelming.

Sometimes we don't even realize why we are so into creating that feeling but our soul wants us to have that elevated perspective. It wants us to rise above our own movie so we can see from a higher perspective. It wants us to care about the planet—our sustaining, nurturing home.

Thank you for sharing these fleeting moments with us. We often experienced the wonder of these moments, but we wrote them off. We threw those moments away. We told ourselves that those moments weren't *real*, we told ourselves that you aren't *real*. But, we long for that connection, it is deep within us and even in our busy, mostly disconnected lives, we still seek it. We are drawn to observe, and become saturated with gratefulness.

Dear Mother,

The planet is sooo full of beauty. We feel really lucky to get to live here where everything we need is provided.

Most of us, just want to live in peace and for our future generations to have a chance at an amazing life.

How do you see us ....as humanity?
You must want us here
Do you see us like an adolescent child?
Do you see us - in partnership?
Do you want us here because it's possible for us to have a relationship with you?

If we can wake up and live in connection with you, maybe we can find a way to live here—in this Garden of Eden—even with all our modern conveniences and creations.

Nature is so perfect—and yet, nature doesn't needs to know what to do, it trusts the perfection of what happens all around us. We see this perfection in everything: from the way our planet dangles in the universe to how the land, the air and the water sustains all life. We see it in how plants grow from seeds into food and then produce new seeds.

The sheer physical beauty of nature is another demonstration and we can feel the energy of nature that invites us to slow our frequencies, connect, and rest in the flowers, the mountains and the grass. Nature is showing us to surrender into trust, to align, connect, receive, and be in relation with the way of the flowers, the flight of the albatross, the flow of the ocean and the communion with all life.

We are going to try. We are going to try to live in a connected way so that our thoughts, our intentions, and our consciousness can undo some of the harm we have created. In this way, we can facilitate healing across the planet. We hope that if more of us can see you as our beautiful, living mother, then we can co-exist and actually experience heaven—here on Earth.

Dear Mother,

Indigenous Peoples around the world had an innate knowing of you as —Mother.

They were so much more connected than we are. They lived in an Ecology, not an Economy. They had a culture where they had an intimate relationship with you, and a respect for all life.

They must have felt a deep connection with you during their ceremonies of powerful drumming—chanting—prayer.

I wonder—did you feel the connection …with them?

It seems like the way they reached out to you would "get through" to you. It must have felt nice for you to have a relationship rooted in respect with that many connected people.

There are still small pockets of connected people—the Native Americans, the Mayans, all the First Peoples—aboriginal peoples of the world, holding on to those ways.

Perhaps the parts of us that were disconnected somehow, deep down, feared the parts of those people that were connected. We could see that they had an inner power, an inner strength and a relationship with you that we didn't understand, so we feared it. We tried to destroy it. Overtly and covertly, we damaged and almost wiped out those values and ways of living.

But there is an awakening happening across the planet and we are beginning to value those perspectives and understand how they lived sustainably and in harmony with you for thousands of years.

This journey of humanity is now beginning to show us that we can be in right relation with you, with ourselves and with each other. We are Acknowledging the Knowledge of the indigenous peoples.

You must be proud.

Dear Mother,

It's time for us to wake up and break through.
Break through the crust of our programming and
old beliefs. Wake up to our own responsibilities
and pay attention to what's calling to us.

We can start by acknowledging you, that you are real.
We can start acting like what we think and do matters.
We can let go of old beliefs that no longer serve us.

Maybe *now* is the time.....

A Hopi Elder Speaks

by The Elders Oraibi, Arizona Hopi Nation

You have been telling people that this is the Eleventh Hour.
Now you must go back and tell the people that this is the Hour.
And there are things to be considered:
Where are you living?
What are you doing?
What are your relationships?
Are you in right relation?
Where is your water?
Know your garden.
It is time to speak your Truth.
Create your community.
Be good to each other.
And do not look outside yourself for your leader.
Then he clasped his hands together, smiled, and said,
"This could be a good time!
There is a river flowing now very fast.
It is so great and swift that there are those who will be afraid.
They will try to hold on to the shore.
They will feel they are being torn apart and will suffer greatly.
Know the river has its destination.
The elders say we must let go of the shore, push off into the middle of the river,
keep our eyes open, and our heads above the water.
And I say, see who is in there with you and celebrate.
At this time in history, we are to take nothing personally,
least of all ourselves.
For the moment that we do,
our spiritual growth and journey come to a halt.
The time of the lone wolf is over.
Gather yourselves!
Banish the word 'struggle' from your attitude
and your vocabulary.
All that we do now must be done in a Sacred Manner
and in Celebration.

WE ARE THE ONES WE'VE BEEN WAITING FOR!

Dear Mother,

In Native American culture, the Seventh Generation had a seat at the table as communities made conscious decisions about the future and about caring for the planet. In our current culture, we act as though our future generations will just have to deal with whatever we leave them.

We see the Seventh Generation as some vague idea far off in the future.

But the truth is, we should each be taking personal responsibility for "our" seventh generation. Many families have five living generations— so it's not that much of a stretch to imagine your actual seventh generation. When we think about it this way, it becomes much more personal, much more specific, and makes us more responsible as we take "the future" into account in our relationship with the planet.

I wonder what the Seventh Generation would say to us?

LETTER FROM THE SEVENTH GENERATION

What were you thinking?

Did you think you could use all the natural resources?

What did you need them for? We have very little to work with here.
We at least hope you used them wisely.

We hope you had some magnificent intent.
We hope that you used all the fossil fuels for some grander vision of what humanity can be.

Please tell us you made conscious decisions about this, and that you used the natural
resources of the planet at least with the idea of making the planet better.

Did you think you could contaminate all the water on the planet?

Please tell us why you thought that was okay.
We have very little clean water left and our historians and earth scientists lead us to believe
that you had vast quantities of clean water—that you could drink straight from any natural
spring or stream.

Please tell us there is a really good reason to contaminate all the fresh drinking water on
the planet.

Did you need to contaminate the water to protect against an alien invasion?
Did you do it to assure the survival of future generations at your own expense?
We know there must have been a really good reason—please help us understand.

Did you think that there was somehow new air being constantly created?

You must have believed that there was always more air being imported into
the atmosphere.

It's the only logical reason we can come up with as to why you polluted the air we breathe. Our science leads us to believe that you could go outside and breathe fresh clean air without a purifier.

We understand that you did what you thought you had to do to survive, so we forgive you for ruining the air. We just wish we understood your rationale. We don't understand what the driving force was or why you felt like you needed to destroy the atmosphere.

There must have been good reasons for damaging the air, water and all the natural resources, but what about our food?

We are left with soil that is depleted, farms saturated with pesticides, and plant species that are so genetically mis-modified that they won't sustain life.

Did you need that much food and farmland to feed all the starving people of your time? If so, that is totally understandable and we forgive you for leaving us without the ability to grow enough food to sustain us.

Looking back at you - from seven generations in the future

We love you.
We thank you.
We forgive you.

We know that you did your very best for us.

Thank You
Your great-great-great-great-great-grandchildren

Dear Mother,

We really don't want to get that letter from our seventh generation. There are choices we can make right now that can change the outcome. The good news is that many of us are waking up. The bad news is we are waking up to a tipping point—or maybe we should view it as a turning point. We can now clearly see that the problems of our world are not going to be solved by politics, governments or religions. We have to look at ourselves and reassess our understanding of who we are, what we want to be, and how we affect our world. It's almost like there are two "models," or beliefs. The Old Model is tired and rooted in separation and it has brought us to this tipping point of destruction. But we are becoming aware of a New Model of us that acknowledges that we are energy, acknowledges our connectedness, and acknowledges the incredible power we are…as individuals.

We have been raised in this old model where we are taught to believe that we are simply a body living in a clockwork, mechanical world. We think that we end, where our skin ends. We believe that everything that is going on inside us—sensations, thoughts and emotions—is contained within our bodies. We think that our inner monologue and the way we feel—affects only us. We believe that we are self-contained—discreet and separate from everything else in the universe.

But a new model is emerging that is showing us that we are One Energy. We can even measure our energy field and it extends well beyond our skin. Further, it turns out that our energy field changes with our thoughts and emotions. Our thoughts are Energy, our emotions are Energy and we are part of the larger energy field of all life. We are becoming aware of how our own energy field extends beyond our skin and how our energy moves through time and space, moves through this plane, this life…. and we begin to notice how it interacts with other energy fields. We are becoming aware of how our energy affects the field around us. In this new model we are connected. We are not separate and we are not self-contained.

We are broadcasting with our thoughts, feelings and emotions.

The part of us that extends beyond our skin interacts with and affects everything and this model shows that we are creative life forces and that we are bigger, more relevant and more powerful than we ever imagined.

When we are aware of this, we are different. When we are *aware* ….everything changes.

Dear Mother,

We are ready to explore how things might be different if we can be more aware of how our energy field lives in this plane. This is a new time in the river of Life - for humanity.

We are remembering that we are energy beings—
We are Energy Being Human, Human Being Energy

Whatever energy comes into us is affected and amplified by our own heart. If neutral energy comes into us from the field, and we are thinking/feeling in a negative way, then the energy that leaves us is negative. But if neutral energy comes into us and we are coming from love and gratitude, then the energy that leaves us is changed, charged and amplified by our internal generator—our heart.

This is our job as a human being. We all affect and co-create the energy field in which we live—through what we think and how we feel. If we could all come more from love and gratitude, imagine what might happen. Our thoughts and feelings are energy.

THE
FIELD

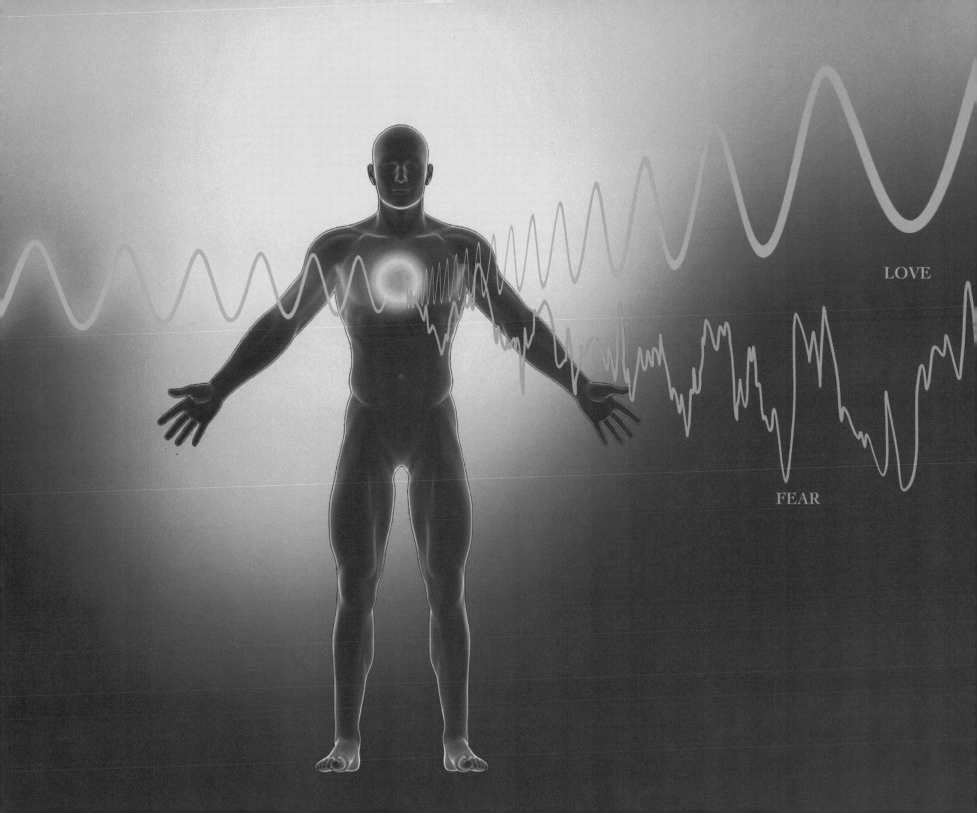

In every moment, our thoughts are affecting the people around us.
We have the ability to choose our thoughts, but sometimes we don't.
We just go on auto-pilot.

But when we connect to our self, our heart, our inner-knower
Our thoughts seem to come from a higher perspective
The more inner we go, the more expanded we are.

If we can choose to broadcast our thoughts with awareness
If we only knew how much affect they have —
Then we might really make a shift.

Our thoughts create our perspective, and our perspective shifts the energy field.
And when the energy field shifts, everything shifts with it.

We are beginning to understand how everything is connected.
We feel the energy of nature
We feel how we are connected to other people, and to all life
We are beginning to understand how important it is that we tend our own thoughts
We are understanding that our thoughts are sacred.

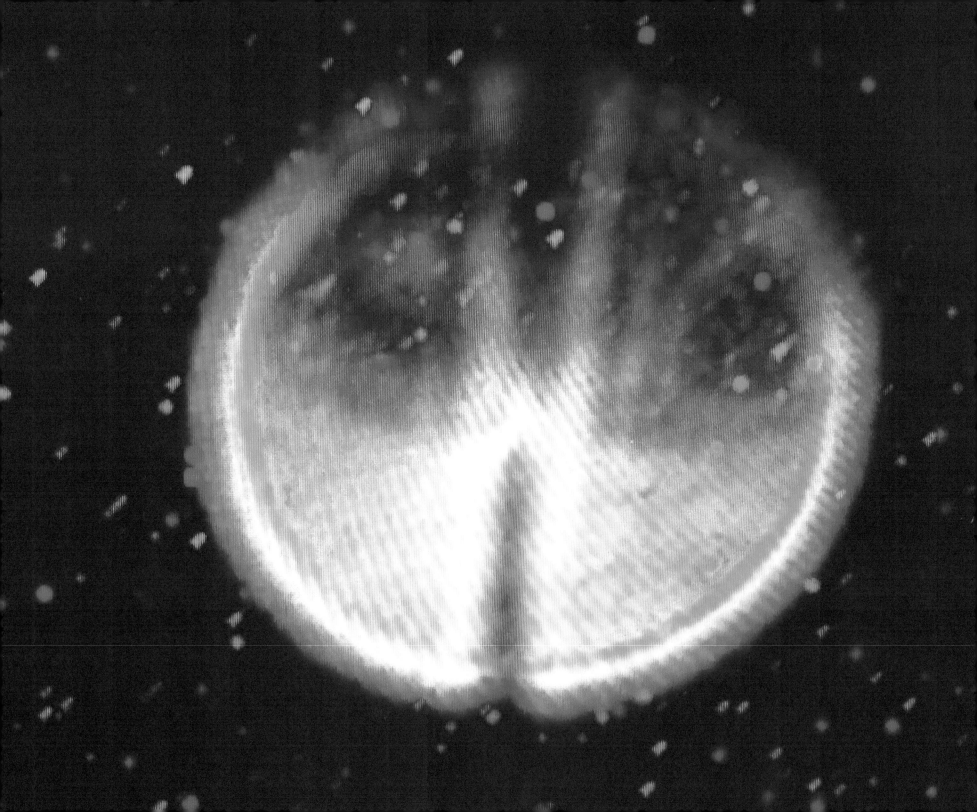

Awareness

In awareness, one feels
The vibration of nature

Living in living ecosystems
Of plants, birds, trees and life
We come to know nature's energy
It accepts us into its fabric

We come to know it
It comes to know us

We are in relation
With the life around us
We grow in appreciation

When we are away from it
We miss it

When we are away from it
It misses us

Dear Mother,

If we want to raise the consciousness of our world, it starts by raising our own consciousness. We can raise the consciousness of our thoughts simply by running them by our inner-knower—our heart. But we have to find our hearts, and we have to remember where we experience connection.

We have lived mostly in our minds
But the place we connect is in our hearts

Our hearts are on a different vibration than our minds
Connection happens on the heart vibration
We feel connection in our heart
The part of the fleeting moment that feels real
Is from the heart

We want to find our own heart
Connect with it and live less in the movie in our mind
and more in our hearts vibration

Give ourselves some space to follow our heart,
Our truth …it's what our soul wants

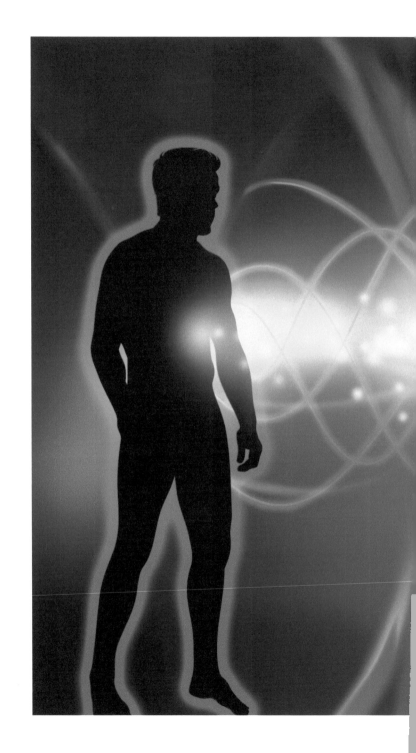

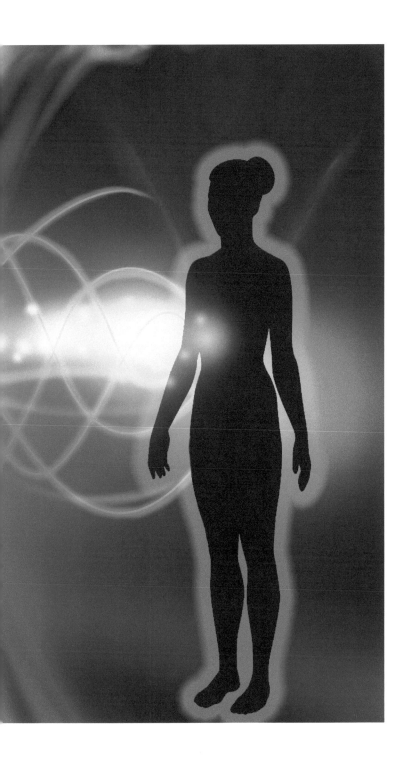

When we come from our heart
Our whole value system changes
It changes what we believe is important

The energy that stems from our hearts
Is a very powerful energy
An enormous life force within the Universe

We experience connection in our hearts and
We experience feelings in our heart.
We are constantly broadcasting our feelings and
We are constantly receiving the energy of others.

The energy we broadcast with our feelings …
has a tangible effect - on everything
What would happen if we transmitted less from our
minds and more from our hearts … with Love?

We have to find our hearts, and
Learn to Live, Lead and Love …from our hearts

The water in me
sees the water in you

The water in me
knows the water in you

The water in me …
is the water in you

Dear Mother,

Not only are we connected to everything by energy—we are also connected by water. The planet is mostly water, our bodies are mostly water, and ….. it's all the same water. Our bodies are made up of the same oxygen, carbon, hydrogen as you Mother—we are the same stuff.

Water is so beautiful, and it's the simplest, most fundamental element that supports all life.

Science is now showing us how our thoughts and our energy can influence water.

Dr. Masaru Emoto has captured stunning photographs of newly frozen water crystals. His photographs show us that when we are thinking positive thoughts, for example, sending the water love and gratitude, the crystals become bright, beautiful, symmetrical, complete, and crystalline. When we don't acknowledge the water, or think negative thoughts, it freezes with dark, chaotic, and incomplete crystals.

The water that we are made of and the water that the earth is made of … is affected by what we think. It's amazing that our energy field actually changes the make-up of water.

Indigenous cultures believe that water has memory, and it retains what it has seen and experienced. Most of our drinking water is kept for long periods in dark tanks and underground pipes, and only sees light of day it sees is when it comes out of the tap. We can help bring that water back to life by simply letting it sit in the room and acclimate to our intention and our energy.

We are connected to the earth. Our bodies are energy wave generating machines, constantly transmitting waves from our words, our thoughts and our emotions.

Our thoughts go out into the energy field, and the waves we put out meet the energy field of everything …and then, literally, everything changes.

If we were all transmitting and receiving in a positive, grateful state of mind each day, our ripple of beautiful, shiny, perfect, healthy water—charged with love and positive intentions—might just create an energetic wave of healing across the planet.

Dear Mother,

If we are having such a profound impact on everything around us, with just the thoughts and the energy we transmit - then maybe we should be more careful and more aware of what we are creating. More aware of our inner self.

The energy that's in our world right now is not that healthy. The unconscious energy we are putting out, is creating what we are experiencing - it's creating our problems. And when we compare our energy, as humanity, to the energy of nature … the energy of nature seems beautiful and nurturing. It feels like the energy of nature is holding a balance and off-setting some of our negative, destructive energy.

Maybe nature is having a hard time balancing us. It feels like our energy is getting out of control and nature is getting tired.

The fix starts with us.

When we start to tune into our own self, our energy, we realize that it originates inside us - in our heart. That place within us is our true is-ness. It's where we feel our connection to the energy of the Infinite. It's our unique ray of the extension of the Infinite and it's affected by every thought we think. Not only is it Affected, but it Affects. It's where it all begins - the Heart of the Matter - the Heart of Us

We are in awe of the vastness, the immensity of "outer space" - but what if our "inner space" is equally vast, equally immense, equally unexplored? We bravely travel into "outer space" but we seem to barely behold, in our human nature, what might be "in there" in our "inner space". But the inner infinity is aware and it's immensity comprehends it's relationship to the infinite. The In-Finite meeting the Infinite.

On some level, maybe we chose to be here - in this plane. To experience the magic. We just have to take care of the magic. If we can maintain that hold on the consciousness of magic, even in this fearful body that thinks it's in separation … it changes the whole vibration of matter here.

The Mother is birthing and emerging and renewing constantly … and here we are … all connected. There is no … staying the same. Everything is in constant motion. When we are open and allowing, we are in attendance of this energy that we are holding. We are temporary vessels here and we have been gifted the ability to Feel, Appreciate and Love and like water, the more we love our own self, our own unique ray of the infinite - the shinier it gets.

Because we are connected - when we tune into our body, we can hear what the Earth is needing and feeling. It's the same with us. We have to tune in and feel our relationship with our own self.

Instead of thinking about what has to be fixed "out there" - we can tune in and constantly broadcast positive thoughts and love.

The answers are so much simpler than what our minds make us chase after. We can just be Minding our Blissness.

We can either view humanity as this crumpled old man, dying with the negative thoughts he was programmed with OR we can choose to view humanity as a new born soul, a fresh slate - with eyes for expansion, openness, connection and love.

It is a Choice.

Dear Mother,

We, your sons, have seen enough
We've been blowing it
Knowing it
We've been too much in the men-tality of
Fighting—for others
Acquiring—for ourselves
And preserving—old ways that aren't working that well.

We have been living disconnected—as individuals in
Disconnected towns and cities
Run by disconnected governments and archaic institutions.

We've been feeling like—there must be a better way.

We have been programmed to be only half of who we are
For some reason, it's difficult for us men to find our hearts
To get to a place of compassion—
Because we've been programmed to view it as a weakness.

But that old programming is leading us right into destruction.
We have to step into right relation.

We are ready to stand up
Be in partnership with women,
Reach in—and take responsibility—for our self.

We have to make a choice (preferably a conscious choice)
to either:
        Stay on the path we have been on - or
        Find a better way.

The path we're on - seems kind of comfortable sometimes
We mostly have jobs, kids, houses, mortgages, distractions
But we don't look at what's really happening to the planet
We see it like this—
If I start to care about the planet,
Then I'm going to have to give something up.
But it doesn't have to be that way.
If we don't take care of the planet,
We aren't going to have to worry about "giving something up"

We sometimes just live in an old belief
Without really viewing it from a higher perspective
And looking at what we believe in our heart.
We have an old story that says its okay to kill each other
for the sake of old beliefs.

We have a responsibility to weigh in here, each of us
We can't just blow this one off ….there's too much at stake.

We have to find our Selves, find our hearts
And decide if we are going to take responsibility …
…or not

It's not even like "having to" take responsibility is a bad thing
We should say, we "get to" take responsibility.

We *get to* create, from an authentic place
A heart-centered place

You *get to* be whoever you are
Just *be* that …with heart

Women seem to come with open hearts
Their open hearts want to connect to an open heart
And live in that space.

We have to find our hearts and open our hearts.

Turn down the volume in our minds and bring
Our attention to our hearts.

It will make a shift
It may be The Shift.

Our future selves would probably kick our ass
If they saw us trying to blow this off:
"Ahh - doesn't sound worth it to me Jim."

It seems crazy to *not* be willing to spend five minutes a day
Connecting to our own heart.
Once we do—we will want to spend more time there
Come from that place in everything we do
It raises our vibration.
Raises our consciousness.

We are an enormous life force
A collective energy … steering the boat

This will take us where we say we want to go.
We have to lead ourselves, and others
When we crack our heart open
It's going to have an effect
Not only on you
But everyone around you.

We want leaders who are heart-centered.

So …. we need to be a leader
In The Shift.

Opening your heart is not a weakness
It's your … heart, your soul, the foundation of you
Your heart feels, Your heart knows
Your heart is where you connect …. to everything, and
Its kind of a critical part of the physical you.

Wouldn't we want to be as connected to our heart as possible?

Think how things would be different if we all made a
conscious choice… If we opened our hearts and lived from there.

Our minds play back all the old ideas of why it
won't work, and how part of us sees it as—weak
The truth is we will be more present and we will be
stronger when we come from our heart.
We will be a force.

The worst of us comes out when our hearts are closed,
and the best of us comes out when our hearts are open.
Atrocities, hate crimes, genocide and cruelty don't
originate in open hearts.

We have to check what our minds are telling us
Check our thoughts
Then change our thoughts, when we need to.

Why not?

We need a new paradigm—a new view of who we are.

It's easy to see ourselves as part of a family, a community,
a region, or even something as big as an entire nation.
But for some reason, it's difficult for us to see
ourselves as a global humanity
As People of the Earth.

We don't usually think of it that way
We've let ourselves get divided into
Smaller and smaller circles
Skin color, religious beliefs, social class, politics,
national boundaries and
Now we are even divided, defined and damaged by which
news we watch and our ideas about the Earth.

There are those who think it's okay to damage the Earth
There are those who want to protect the Earth

It seems crazy that this is even a discussion.

Remember—
We have free will
We *get to* decide
We're not just along for the ride.

We are supposed to be leaders, protectors, warriors
Be a warrior of change—not a warrior brother against brother.

We have to change the game.

Let's not get divided and fall into a civil war with each other
There is no such thing as a civil war.

Brother—we are an enormous force
We are going to work—as a family of humanity—
to make this right.

This is real.

Dear Mother,

Thank you for letting us, your daughters, come into this physical world with the innate gentle nurturing that is our feminine essence—unconditional, nurturing, preserving, accepting and allowing, like you. We have a relationship with the feeling of love in our hearts.

But change is happening. The river of life is moving fast now, and we need to become more responsible for preserving the true nature of the feminine—aware of the inner relationship in our hearts and responsible for nurturing and preserving all that we have received.

Some of us feel like we are having to be more independent… to play both roles, the masculine and the feminine, and put on the mask of the masculine.

But as we step up and step in—to the culture created by man—we want to maintain our feminine awareness and appreciation for our openness. We want to hold onto our relationship we have cultivated with our hearts. We want to pay attention to our energy and not fall into the world created by the demands of our current culture. We don't want to lose the openness and gentleness of our nature. We hope our hearts will remain open to connection and one-ness.

So much of the manmade world of politics, advertising, and news has made us want to contract and push away. We thought we were less, thought we weren't pure love, thought we had to "get" love. We thought we had to be a certain way to have a sense of value. We followed the path of the mind of man. But as we walk down a new path, we don't want to leave behind that sense of openness that the feminine …. is.

Imagine if the feminine essence was lost in the world.

We are the keepers. The Mother of All Life has entrusted that with us.

We have to be in partnership with men, and stay open, maintaining our own sense of relationship with love. We will not lose the foundation of unconditional love that you have shown us.

The masculine is working to open their hearts. The feminine is trying not to let theirs close.

We are needing to remember to appreciate the power and the value of the feminine.

The highest octave of the Feminine is Universal Love. The highest octave of the Masculine is Universal Knowledge. When we bring them together—with no resistance, no polarization—that is the whole essence of creation. To come from a place of no separation, from a field of love.

The grandmothers encourage us to look up towards a higher way or a higher perspective. We know that we all carry our ancestors' and our grandmothers' DNA within us. Maybe that's why this message speaks to us so clearly.

Message from the Grandmothers

A breeze is stirring. Feel the sun on your wings.

As you move through these changing times.. be easy on yourself and be easy on one another... You are at the beginning of something new. You are learning a new way of being. You will find that you are working less in the yang modes that you are used to. You will stop working so hard at getting from point 'a' to point 'b' the way you have in the past.. but will instead spend more time experiencing yourself in the whole and your place in it. Instead of traveling to a goal out there.. you will voyage deeper into yourself.

Your mother's mother's mother knew how to do this. Your ancestors from long ago knew how to do this. They knew the power of the feminine principle and because you carry their DNA in in your body.. this wisdom and this way of being is within you. Call on it.. call it up. Invite your ancestors in. As the yang based habits and the decaying institutions on our planet begin to crumble.. look up. A breeze is stirring. Feel the sun on your wings.

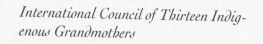

International Council of Thirteen Indigenous Grandmothers

Dear Mother,

We have so much to learn from you. I mean—just look at you—you are radiant, brilliant, glowing, beautiful, spectacular. And you have been for billions of years. You are in perpetual motion, constantly renewing—your air, your water, how water falls and washes over the land, flows into rivers, feeds the oceans, moves across the globe on wind currents, evaporates and then is carried back across the land where the rain falls and starts the cycle over again. This perpetual cleansing and sustaining has happened continuously for millions of years. It's how we can breathe the same air as the dinosaurs and the drink the same water that has always been here. You are always cleansing and renewing.

We didn't hurt you, our home ~ on purpose.
We didn't hurt each other either ~ on purpose.
We created out of unawareness and disconnectedness, and caused harm to ourselves, to each other and to you.
We did it unconsciously—creating out of handed-down beliefs, and old programming.
Our collective past convinced us that hurting and killing each other was okay.

The energy from these thoughts and feelings is getting heavy. We can let go—cleanse these negative thoughts and experiences through forgiveness and openness. We can learn not to hold onto energy from old thoughts, words, and deeds. Mother, you don't hold onto stagnant energy and neither should we. You are always sustaining and nurturing life. Your processes are perpetually in motion, cleansing and creating anew.

We will forgive ourselves, forgive all people and let go of old beliefs that no longer serve us.

World Heart Affirmation
by Howard Wills

For All Humanity
The Earth And All Life
Throughout All Time
Let's All Forgive Each Other, Forgive Ourselves
Love Each Other And Love Ourselves
Now And Forever
Please And Thank You
Thank You

Dear Mother,

Mother—we think we got it now. We love you and thank you for all the beauty in our lives and how you have helped us to get us to this point—the point where we can take responsibility for ourselves. We know that our thoughts matter and that we can be more aware of how our thoughts affect everything around us. We are also aware that the feeling of connection is in our hearts. We can imagine what life would be like—and how much more amazing our lives would be—if we were all living from a place of harmony, full connection and love.

We are Surviving in our disconnectedness, but we could be Thriving in our connection.

Mother—excuse us—maybe we need to talk to ourselves here for a minute.

Our collective Selves know all this is true. That we can't continue to treat the planet like one big resource for us to acquire and use. We are of the Earth, not on the Earth.

We have lulled ourselves to sleep. We have fallen into a system where we just follow old stories and beliefs without even questioning where we are heading. We are on autopilot. But there has to be a part of us that knows. Our inner knower. Our internal compass will be helping us navigate our way out of this old story.

The only solution is from the inside out.
We have to allow ourselves to come from a place of appreciation
A place of love—then
Everything starts to change
We start to perceive differently
We start to think differently
We start to feel differently.

Maybe we should really get to know ourselves. Feel from the part that's inside us—that we haven't been paying attention to.

We *know* it's there—but sometimes it's just easier to just push on. Pretend like its not real. But we have experienced fleeting moments of connection. The part of us that feels—is *real*.

And if it's real—then, wouldn't we want to get to know it?

It is *you*.
It's the part of you that's connected to everything.

If you connect to that part of you, it will expand you. Because you are
connected to everything: Mother Earth, Father Sky and The Creator.

And from that place of connection you can make conscious decisions about your life.

Let your heart lead and your mind follow.

If we all were to make conscious decisions about our lives, just imagine the possibilities. We could re-write the whole story. It can be anything we can imagine.

Maybe we can turn things around. Maybe we can remember how it used to be—when we lived in connection and in appreciation with the spirit of Mother Earth. And maybe we can use our technologies and modern conveniences in balance and harmony.

The possibilities are really exciting!

If we could take a poll of humanity, I wonder what 98% of us really want in life. People all over the world really just want to get along with their neighbors and provide for their children. It's odd that we unconsciously go along with letting 2% of us create wars and propagate old beliefs.

What is our plan for existing long term on this planet? There doesn't seem to be any type of global conversation about it - about how humanity can exist here. We have no strategic plan. Each country could tell you their plan, which would probably be full of ideas about expanding their economy, their Gross National Product. But if that is the plan for every government, in every country—how could that be consistent with our real need to sustain human life on Planet Earth?

It's odd we don't look at it like that.

Mother, one way we can begin to get a glimpse of what is possible is to simply look at nature. There are so many lessons you have shown us. The answers are all around us. Nature seems to be very good at allowing life to guide it into balance, perfection, and the kind of harmony that has allowed life to thrive on this planet for billions of years. All life on the planet just knows what to do. We have convinced ourselves that we are separate from nature—so, we experience separation.

The programming of separation through history is deep. It goes way back into our ancestry. It's a little scary to think that the programming is hundreds of generations deep, and that begs the question: will it take hundreds of generations to undo the programming?

The good news is that the programming can't really stand up. It's not the truth, and therefore, the programming is coming unraveled very quickly. What has taken hundreds of generations to instill begins falling apart as soon as it is exposed to the light of truth. Our youth are waking up in less than one generation. There is hope. This is truly exciting.

In addition, we are living in a time when it's so much easier to disseminate information. We literally have the world at our fingertips. We are super-charged by the internet. Dogma doesn't hold up with peoples' access to information, especially when people gain access to their own hearts.

Mother—we may need a vision, an idea, an inspiration as to what life can
be like once we are living in full connection. It might help us take those
final steps and be diligent in letting go, in tending our thoughts, in remembering
that what we think about matters, and in acting like we are all one.
As individuals, we can start with what we can control
What we think
How we feel
How we relate and
How we perceive.

We can all wake up to find our specific purpose
This can be a transformative shift, raising our consciousness.

As a global humanity
We are an Enormous life force.
Powerful, even in the spectrum of the Universe.

The higher heart frequency of love is coming in.
Having a crystalline affect on our energy.
The vibration of what we broadcast… is affecting matter.

Humanity has the key
Our mind is awakening
Our thoughts are becoming clear
We will be creating from a different place
It's up to us.

When we think and speak the thoughts and desires of the heart—
out loud—we create a frequency that affects our energy field and
creates our reality.

We know we have to unlock the real power of our hearts and minds.

Why wouldn't we? There is too much at stake. We are at stake!

Friend do it this way - that is,
whatever you do in life,
do the very best you can
with both your heart and mind.

And if you do it that way,
the Power Of The Universe
will come to your assistance,
if your heart and mind are in Unity.

When one sits in the Hoop Of The People,
One must be responsible because
All of Creation is related.
And the hurt of one is the hurt of all.
And the honor of one is the honor of all.
And whatever we do affects everything in the universe.

If you do it that way - that is,
if you truly join your heart and mind
as One - whatever you ask for,
that's the Way It's Going To Be.

~ WHITE BUFFALO CALF WOMAN ~

About the Authors

Rick Ferguson is a lifelong environmentalist. He spent the first part of his life in the technical field as a geological engineer studying the physical nature of the Earth. He formed an environmental engineering company in the 90s and spent his working career cleaning up some of the most technically complex sites on the planet.

The second part of his life put him on a spiritual path when he had a profound experience with a tree while trail running in the woods of East Tennessee. His route would take him to the top of a ridge, where he would climb into his favorite tree and, for the most part, have a one-way conversation. Over time, he learned to slow his frequency to match the ancient spirit of this majestic, grandfather tree so that he could truly recognize the tree, connect with it, appreciate it, share his story and "tune in" to the tree's own story. He developed a relationship with the tree and ultimately the tree gave him the name Spirit Walker …because he had the spirit of the trees but could walk the talk and move around the earth to bring awareness to the consciousness of nature.

That experience called him to write these Letters to Mother. He reasoned that if an individual tree could have consciousness, then surely the entire planet has consciousness, and he began to explore his relationship with Mother Earth.

Malana Fiore contributed immensely to the content, story, and tone of these letters as a co-creator. She is a spiritual mentor and she personifies the Divine Feminine …living, teaching and relating from the space of unconditional love, nurturing and teaching. She has extensive knowledge of the Cards of the Magi and she teaches this "language of the soul" on Kauai - www.magiguild.com. Malana's wisdom was a true gift to the development of this book, and her understanding of this deeper language is a gift to humanity …waiting to be fully realized. Her ability to relate to Spirit and mastery of this language has led her to some deep understandings reflected in these letters about connecting to our inner-knower, tending our thoughts, and simply minding our blissness.

Photo Credits

Cover Ramberg/istock.com

p3   © Alex Maxim/maximimages.com

p7   Moon with a View

p9   Smileus/bigstock.com

p11   Serge Bertasius Photography/depositphotos.com

p13   Aleksandar Mijatovic/shutterstock.com

p15   Antartis/depositphotos.com

p17   Samuel Silitonga/pexels.com

p20   Pellinni/Depositphotos.com

p21   Matthias Mullie/unsplash.com

p23   Jesse Zheng/EyeEm/gettyimages.com

p25   Gloria Glo Designs/gloriaglo.com

p39   xload/depositphotos.com

p47   Kevron2002, destinacigdem/depositphotos.com

p50   PopTika/shutterstock.com

p52   National Geographic photographer, Charles O' Rear

p56   Brandon Jean/unsplash.com

CPSIA information can be obtained
at www.ICGtesting.com
Printed in the USA
BVHW060601111219
566144BV00002B/3/P